Accidental Animals

MICHAEL TRUSSLER

HAGIOS PRESS

Copyright © 2007 Michael Trussler

Library and Archives Canada Cataloguing in Publication

Trussler, Michael Lloyd, 1960-
   Accidental animals / Michael Trussler.

Poems.
ISBN 978-0-9739727-8-8

   I. Title.

PS8639.R89A63 2007   C811'.6   C2007-904741-6

Edited by Don Coles.
Designed and typeset by Donald Ward.
Cover painting: *Grip* by Shayne Brandel, oil on canvas, 84" x 84" (artist represented
   by the Art Ark Gallery, Kelowna, BC, www.theartark.com/brandel.html).
Back cover photo by Amy Snider.
Cover design by Yves Noblet.
Set in Adobe Caslon Pro.
Printed and bound in Canada.

The publishers gratefully acknowledge the assistance of the Saskatchewan Arts Board, The Canada Council for the Arts, and the Cultural Industries Development Fund (Saskatchewan Department of Culture, Youth & Recreation) in the production of this book.

HAGIOS PRESS
Box 33024 Cathedral PO
Regina SK   S4T 7X2

amy

Contents

Loves

Conversations

In the likeness of what animal was the world made?

Plato
Timaeus

A POEM FOR MY DAUGHTER

Annie, it's true that you make poems, but
the thing is, each new time
you never know
how —
        Easier, by far,
to tell stories, recall your body
in your nightgown the night I asked
you what story you wanted me to read, and you
pressed up against me as you turned off
the light because you wanted me
to make one up instead / because in
that kind of story anything can happen, you said, and you can
change what happens, change
what happens —

Darling Annie, if only Daddies could change what happens when
changing what happens is
what they ache most to do.

Because I don't know how old
you are, just now, as you read this —

Think of the happy guy you see
in a steakhouse / he's just been paid, he's wearing
a soft suit the colour of Japanese
holy water, he's a man with fresh breath, a man
who knows a woman loves him, a man who is
equally at home
with a clown driving down the street
in the world's smallest car / and the secrets
women want to trade with each and every
mirror the face is. Sometimes

poems are like that.

Look at me. Let me see you
seeing me.

I want to write so many things all at once, but
can only offer a string of paper
flamingoes lifting off just
as dusk happens / think of them
during the hours taking
place inside you

the first time you do drugs / and also when
I'm gone and you wear a pair
of reading glasses strung
across your breasts.

When you were a child I wore as many masks
as I could imagine to entertain you / and a poem
is this mask, or that one, and then
another,
        one which can only be heard, perhaps
touched, but not seen.

Listening to your magic, Annie, some sounds
can change into
other sounds: a dragonfly (one
of the largest, its wingspan outreaching a sparrow's, its abdomen
holding perfectly formed chips
of blue paint)
        jaywalks
through the air, its movement the thin rustle of leaves
in the crazy-glue sunlight
of autumn. But some sounds are

somewhere only themselves: a hot
air balloon, its burst
of sudden flame passing over precisely
where it is
you are
Annie.

CONTORTIONS

is her pageant, the generous woman down the street
with her garden gnomes, and Dutch kids who disappear
into the garage at night, still
kissing. There's some bluebirds nailed
to her trees, two wishing wells, various other animals, some
watering actual flowers who live beneath a tribe
of smiling spiders. From May
to September, two more kids stay on a frozen swing,
impossible to steal during any hour of the year.

　　　Then the scarecrows come, the
vampires, mummies, and then several Santa
Clauses, the wise kings, shepherds and candy canes.

Depending upon the season, skeletons, small, revering
cows, and even smaller leprechauns, but never
once a woodland nymph. She's
grateful when someone
praises the show but
that's not the point. Anyone

can decorate a lawn. She wants
to tell us something / because at night she's
stood on the lawn, stood
there naked except for
the flame.

THE BLUE BALL

It would take about one and a half
crows wing-to-wing to surround
its circumference — the blue
ball on the grass. Twilight, a prairie

lawn, and the ball's an unscratched
mirror holding stark and bluest
trees, a small arch of sky, the house
steady behind me, but not
my son. He's over
there, way over there, in primary colours, rubber boots,
two hands on the garden hose, he's playing
at good work, playing firefighter, even playing
at being me. I ask him to come give the ball
a drink, and then he's off
again, bending over to

take in the pleasure of water and the invisible
spiders that water and mud
make. The ball uncurves
its vista fresh again, a miniature exempt
from geometry's collisions, the home
that can't ever be met
for the first time.

2.
Because the ball is more
than any woman a siren, because
the unjourneyed world only
lying on its skin wants me
to discard everything, I step

back, regain the pale shuffling
of actual dimensions and my son's
hardly there
                 I see him
a mirage as if at the mind's edge. He's abandoned
to purpose and I wander

3.
around the yard, touching a spruce
he sprayed earlier, force my
eye along the lemon of a warbler on the back fence, the bird
granting sudden lineage to the wood's
cracked paint. I shoot an entire roll

of film, some of it in colour, some
in black and white, some in surrender
and this condenses the entire
thickening world down —

a patch of skin
swabbed by a nurse just before the needle. And we,
this world's unguarded skin, are its
rainy breath, its always changed

upon blood / and we choose
its wind-stretched
light.

in the curl of her arm chair my Pentecostal grandmother
flew through her Alzheimer's like a parrot
back to her century's beginnings. Flew past the gray-crayoned
hours, back to before work and long womanhood, flew through silver
spoons, past summer's inward bridges, flew back to a point
before Satan started watching
from his corners.

Pears were for eating. Then steaming and canning.

Then finally something shaped like a ball.

But there were no children. Where are the children?

When she'd awaken, minutes would arrive like alien chopsticks from
    a place
she'd never visited. Food became unusual and then empty, not good
for much at all.

She'd only seen a parrot once. It was a jeweled Ukrainian egg.

She's known beads that were real, and something that looked like a
    heart
made of amethyst, a word she'd
never learned. In the back of her house
there was a dark and crowded space
with a block of wood
and an axe.

This is where she killed chickens for supper.

The earth floor was damp with an enameled smell, her apron
the colour of fish in a field of wheat.

Flashes of sound. Few.

Flashes of sound. None. All

in one place, all in one

place.

But that, near the end, she ceaselessly
polished her fingernails
with her young woman's thumb.

Saturday, April 5

Writing from this bestiary — a shark
closing in on a spray of roses, peach
roses, a sea turtle sliding down
the widened aperture of a box

camera, a chameleon resting on
a thick clump of words —
there's nothing I wouldn't
tell you

if words could give
me your presence.

Saturday, April 12

But first, look
at this nearly empty
page. No, you have
to look much

more closely, the margins
are troubled with things
trying to get in —

some thin pictures from
last week's newspapers.

My eye is so slow. First I saw
the child's arm, a
bandaged stump, and then

there was his other arm, just the same, though
severed higher,
                              the caption mentioning
dead parents, he's 12, which means he was born during
the first desert war. And the same bombs
released a man from jail, his chest made
a parchment by knives, sharpened
screw drivers, some cigarette burns / his
crime: stealing flour from the ruling
Party — he was a baker; he'd
been gone

Saturday April 19

ten years. This week seemed hardly to budge, though
the mutilated boy went on television, the baker
vanished, and inside the other facts, the
casual verities from which
the eye must choose:

tomorrow is this year's Easter, or
a man with a beak curving down (filled
with potpourri) and upraised broad hat
spoke terrible things to me from the end
of his circled world, he's a replica of a Medieval doctor
in a local museum exhibition on microbes
and plagues, or

last week I bought a history of tattoos. Among
the hearts, flowering snakes, sometimes beaming
icons, and the extraordinary number of skulls, an artist
from Samoa gave someone's skin perfectly
tasting panty hose from knee to eternal
thigh / another had sewn diane

arbus's photo "Child with a toy
hand grenade in Central Park, N.Y.C.
1962" onto a young man's
right arm. But poems are separate
insurrections,
                not light, not
history, not skin.

Passover

If only to hear one voice —
An angel's.

To learn why and how or when
the page quicksands

into even more of more
uninterrupted white upon

damned and unwavering
white.

IRAQ: OPERATION SHOCK AND AWE, THE NEW SUBLIME

I wish Kant could have seen
the stranger down the hall, the one
watching CNN today, the one getting
turned on taking in the computer's
night-scope-green, this new light

making way for bright mossy tanks, rapid
spectral men — the so many
desert machines.

                      Both hands
wrapped around the computer screen, she's
a believing Christian, an even fiercer
mother of two, a boy, a girl, still
babies mostly, which means

nothing / neither love
nor God ever
altered anyone.

What's really important
is this:
                she knows the correct names
for all the weaponry, can identify
each unit of soldiers, hones in
on each target / and she knows, she
knows that she's
part of the team.

PORTRAIT WITH ARBITRARY SCENES
AND ACCIDENTAL ANIMALS

Amidst the most extraordinary fire.

You asked me to choose. Choose between rebellion
and unguarded wonder, burials at sea or
beneath the drum-beaten sky.

So I've been led to gather and scavenge
for things. Examine them.

2.

First with my fingers, from the waist up — these streets falling away
resemble women, I thought. And I learned to see with my stomach,
where the nerves gather, found a run of blue desert — the fixed and
myopic sky — to sit beneath. Sometimes animals came by,
recognizing how I cared about things. The unbroken game back
then being to strike down the need for any kind of deal. Not to give
what's due, neither to Caesar or God — this was to see how the
word *or* suddenly candles beauty amidst our Ptolemaic thinking.

3.

That was twenty years ago, before I knew
that most of them would be spent
living in potent but fake shadows, sometimes overhearing
voices sip at my brain.

In between these twenty years — marriage, doctors, a job worth
keeping, necessary drugs, the dazzle of children, and
now divorce — a useful and fortunate life that hasn't
yet vanished. Or flared.

This remembering everything but not the right things.

4.

A mind that works finds itself an oasis, surveys
from where it's come, is renewed, and then sets off
again, but mine is more like what happened
to Pompeii. From out of nowhere, a muddy and fiery hailstorm
strikes, burying the immediate. Sometimes there are warnings,
but most often, unlike Vesuvius, the storm comes without
being perceived / it doesn't matter, seen or
unseen /   / the damage
remains the same. This isn't to say I completely

regret sudden fire or
cooling ash.

5.

Only this morning a magpie took off from the birdbath, its claws
scratching a sound unlike anything heard
elsewhere /

            and moments before it had raided a sparrow's nest
and won an egg to drink.

The many worlds crammed with spoils.

In between the unopened and accidental round
of days — the point is what? To invent as if to record as if to love as
if to splash quick and formulaic graffiti across
the disregarded slums of the mind?

Perhaps.
Persuade me.

SALVA NOS

One morning in summer a man's ribs opened up
and out came a girl. No, that's not what happened. Instead,
this: once, in a long, and mutable, a carnal summer,

a crow visits.

Flies down from the mast
in the parking lot. Flies down
because she can't resist
an open window, can't keep away
from the plush heart you gave me, the one that
I've tricked her into thinking
is meat. It's only ten

o'clock in the morning, and she's already
pecked July's wet stars from the carpet, shown
me a boy in a blue bottle. *Once, he'd*
pulled a wagon, a red one (as it should
be) and in it a bushel of gray
fire — the immediate and contented ash
of a roaming childhood. It's only ten

o'clock in the morning, and the crow, she's
hidden my wedding ring, leashed
my desire for other people's memories, and just now
she tells me that many floors above
someone's collapsed while washing
last night's dishes. She's

insistent with impossible facts: that each day,
past and future, presses its claims
on this one. And fluttering among

my blow-up dolls — Venus
de Milo, Piet Mondrian, and Ganesh — the crow
finally lands on my robin shell
bed. She's summer incarnate. Its unexpected
stairwells, waving ferns, a moon
made of moss. But up close, her shadow's

a guillotined halo / and as for me, perched
on the shelf of what actually happens, I'm merely

a clump of what's vertical in a season, a space
that's crowded with flight
and emptied of touch.

AT THE CIRCUS TODAY

Sigmund Freud must have invented the circus.
Babylon's beside Barnum repeating the uneven present, and everyone
keeps jumping through rings. After he's already
sacrificed her once in a rocket, the Ringmaster chains a woman inside
a moving doorway. Spread wide, she could be waiting
for Kong. And then, she's sealed away from
the rest of us. The ringmaster taunts
the motorcycle between his legs
before bursting through the doorway
in sparks, exploding paper, and Wagnerian
guitar. The woman needed to be
destroyed again if she's to uncurl once more unharmed
from her velvet box that's glowing with stars
and the rings of Saturn.

2.
I don't know anything about elephants.

But at the circus today, from way, way behind worn down
headgear, and desert folds around her eyes, one
looked at me. She could tell she was
in front of everyone and she was
also breathing in another world

and when she gathered me in her eye my shoes first and then
the rest of me began to disappear. And then
she went around the ring again tagged
to another's tail, her skin a map that kept moving. Her scent rubbed
the popcorn, the green smoke rippling with stage
lightning, the barking crowd, and each

3.

new poem desires to hold fast to reshape different kinds
of love / but then the sudden world occurs, sweeping apart
every street. Because the roar carries us away, throws
anchors down where no one would ever want
to stay, I first had to give

you the circus's falling noise / only now
can you meet the elephant's touch. When she
pushed me down into someplace else, your
fingers came from behind and lifted me, then wafted us

both nearly to the top of the tent. The circus went

on as if we were only
missing, but the elephants drew us
down, gave us

their million wrinkled pathways
to follow / and

4.

it's also true that everything —
everything is done, everything
to avoid rehearsing
the dirty velvet of your
receding voice.

THE CONTORTIONIST

Being a contortionist is enlarging work. It's also
tiring — embellishing the extent
of the literal. Each pose shows her
leaving home. Each pose occurs amidst the fluid
materiality of other people. She's observed skeletons
bursting with their secret lives inside, studied clerks
in sex shops, the past century's stage directions. She's watched
her dentist's fingers, neon signs and bats. Her body
is a love song to St. Sebastian. Her

impossibly raised pubis is an anvil upon which summer's
last butterfly is made. Parallel to ours, her body
contains what escapes memory. Her skin
sometimes glares a car's headlights
sweeping through country roads.

Her repertoire is endless.

Her act has included a man sleeping on pavement. The uncollected
rocks on the moon. A day trip to Auschwitz. Ladders on
toy fire trucks, what dolphins
really think.

Merely to listen, she takes
daily excursions into stairwells. Without an audience, she
scratches her scalp, resolves to eat only carnivores
for a week / without an audience /

her body's knowledge
is tireless.

INHERITANCES

Symbol isn't dead; it's a parasite that grows
inside of things. Look at those jade figurines: a bat eating a peach,
Wen Chen holding a brush, a catfish nibbling
immortality's fungus. A rosary, the size
of a squirrel's head, holds a medieval virgin fresh with austerity;
on the reverse,
                   a jawless, jealous skull, its eyes — stained
ivory. Take in too the bloodless
litter of pre-Silurian spirifers, amethyst, drunken
malachite, the several mummies, one
a Ptolemaic woman,
                 kernels of crust for teeth
that once gentled the cock of a seething
man, now
she shares a glass cage with today's dust, and a hawk:
Horus, the one-eyed nobody, avenger
of sin against families.

But oh my henchmen
this myriad room — its eyeglasses, the winding
staircase of Morphic butterflies,
                       the cluttered,
jangling noise of kaas forever discovering
just how precise the afterlife really is.

2.
There are so many species
of failure the consolations
of perception merely vanish,
            even as art abandons
its various companions, leaves each

to untoward death.   Pause
over these Japanese *tsubai*
suspended in their softly lit case,
like pike, like scoured prayers
before sleep — elegant, rapt, impossible
to satisfy.
            Their blades,
unsummoned in lacquered wood,
thinner than the beat of a pulse, their hilts inlaid
with cloud, inexorable peak, and fir.

And one yearns for different things. You become
restless for the present, that amazing
glue to which nothing sticks.

3.
You want windy yellow fences with tacked on shadows / you want
a life like a man walking through a crowd wearing
a maroon tie painted on his shirt / you want the delayed
familiarity of skin.

On a beach you've met strangers
in English, French, even
Russian if need be.
                Wherever you've gone
you've envisioned entrances, a future hoarded with homecomings,
desired return. But memory isn't
a chalice, and indifference
isn't betrayal,
            and every time
you sign your name you've
announced evasion. And then

4.
I've dreamed a certain small town.
We need to drive there together.

At night,
the lights of the police station
are pooled beside
                    the town's library,
and a huge and angry bridge
sways in something like rain.

Park there on the sweating,
earmarked street.

If we spill a dozen bottles
of aspirin over the warm
hood of the car and wait
behind the blurred confetti,
pressing down on the horn
until someone arrives,
                    then
it won't be too late, the world
won't already have
always begun.

ADAM'S THREE DISCOVERIES

    The incision
was closed with the jaws
of decapitated ants,
     the liquor for pain
he gave me flattened my brain
with difficult dreaming of broken
black bodies, but Adam
saw an orgy of angels that made her,
tore from the earth
     her coal dusty skin, drew
her unconscious from the migration
of animals, fluke and eye-mists, sea tracks
untravelled by me. Gem wrung

agate and amethyst, blue
yet mottled, this stranger woven,
sounded from nowhere,
from Adam.

Adam, you shiver of mud and God-spit
touch of a toucan's brain
taste her, sweat her,
     froth, wriggle,
wade a finger and spin her,

but most, wake her into my crowded
conversation of one, and leave
your sleep, leave.

2.

Sunday at the beach. A wing
stuck in the sand. Eve wearing her smile.
God already talking again
the day of the week after:

> *there are eons of sanity and*
> *beside them, a fury of air —*
>
> *your kind will find itself*
> *locked in irony,*
> *like worms bottled*
> *in mescal / there are*
> *other times than the future's*
> *amber past*

        and Adam knew nature missing
him, became adept at simple hallucination, saw
a congress of gulls, one of them
pulling a string from a fish,
a sight he would someday
become used to.

                Closer,
an empty socket, a hole for him to
peer through. The gull's eye, a black
sun, shone on the terribly new.
Adam reeled
        and felt skin tighten
around the voice speaking

> *there's a reptile loose*
> *on the world, a gate of teeth and yesterday,*
> *spikes like yucca leaves, shimmering*
> *with regret's slow alchemy*

and Adam tried imagining death
and God
                              kept talking while Eve —

stretching out beneath a parasol
large and powdery-bright
the size of a foreskin
taken from a sperm whale —

                    already senses the plummet
of recollection.

3.
                    Adam then unpursued,
searches in the wilderness of his nerves
to find just where the hell he
is, thus
                    Adam half-asleep
on horseback, deep in the north
where nihilism grows, past brimstone-butter
flies disappearing
                              into summer's
awful serenity, and Adam
wishes for winter,
                              a hat brimming with snow,
ice poised like a needle
over an unformed tattoo, the trick
of melt-water,
                              but sees instead
someone silent in front of something
impossibly foreign.
                              Adam struggles, crosses
over the plain of his mind, but can't begin

to recognize
the new object — a simple
canvas on an easel.

It was if water
had propped itself straight up, reflecting
what normally passed for sight, but held
and stayed.

Stones began to move, and the water
sprouted vermilion anger where the stranger
touched it, God was nowhere
to be seen.

The painting held his garden
with a dozen Eves, all different,
the one he knew sleeping matched
the breasts the painter made, delighting
Adam into showing the stranger his own trick —

Crooked, crested crane, taffeta slipping,
Adam lanternless, Adam joining

words together, speckled poppy
into zircon, zircon needing
its own unnameable waves,
Adam speaking the tip of everywhere, but

words would never touch
the stranger who
drew a harp

and strung a body through it, made
a shark fornicate with wisdom, an eel

trail menses, and Adam felt
　　　　　he'd stumbled into the backroom
of God's mind before creation.

　　　　　In a flash
　　　　the stranger showed Eve, deaf
like water, like sand, Eve on his gathering
canvas, about to embark
　　　　　on the memory of Cain, whose
eyes, mercury and intolerable spice,
would demand to see
what it was
his parents now knew.

TO MY TWO CHILDREN, WHO WON'T REMEMBER
THE TWENTIETH CENTURY

You came to us
              when this time where most of us have lived was almost
gone and we can never know what is necessary
to tell you —

I was born the year Kennedy became President, which I learned
later
      was a kind of ending. You could say the entire
century was a never-ending parade
of suspended
endings.   Your grandfather
loved JFK and I can still hear the dead god talking to some people
in Berlin on the stereo from Dad's three record set, but
Berlin meant nothing
to me then.

2.
Let me try this another way: there's a painted piano, &
the painter was a man who grew that now

lost century through his finger
tips, and I once sat with the woman I loved before
your mother, sat with her / the piano was
                    mostly white but also holds strips of colour, the story
of creation in tiny blues,
                        green and blazing angels,
and so many glistening people yet to come.

And
the painter was Chagall, and the city is Nice and a hotel on a
cobbled street wears a brass plaque that mentions
how the hotel's rooms

once saw people slowly made
into corpses by Hitler's
police. And now the Internet's showed me
that building in France, its

Pikaia is the missing and final link in our story of contingency — the direct
                        connection between Burgess
paintings' nerves again   and my brain's been slapped
    decimation and eventual human evolution. We need no longer talk of
                        subjects peripheral to our parochial
by an empty wave — what I've forgotten and what I've kept
        concerns. . . . Wind the tape of life back to Burgess times, and let it
                        play again. If *Pikaia* does not survive
burning somehow together as if I've been flushed
        in the replay, we are wiped out of future history — all of us, from
                        shark to robin to orangutan. And I don't
with neon seawater. This, the abandoning
        know that any handicapper, given Burgess evidence as known today,
                        would have granted very favourable
fastenings of memory
                        odds for the persistence of *Pikaia*
                                        Stephen Jay Gould, *Wonderful Life*
is the twentieth century —

which must also be an account
of the mind
            but not only of
the mind

3.

one winter afternoon, take off your socks; go outside, not
to play, but to stand
in the snow. Within seconds, the pain
will start.

　　　We have maps and diagrams

of the place, Treblinka; we can see where the trains dumped
families off, can see the well-used Road to Heaven where everyone
had to wait their turn, naked, in the flattened snow. No one
knows why the world didn't end during those hours
there. Yet　　　　dawn returned
because
it always does.

Treblinka. Hiroshima. Biafra. Argentina. Cambodia. Bosnia.
　　Rwanda.

While it's true that each name ends with the letter *a* / there is
only one fact: the only sacred thing in the universe
is children.

4.

Some things were
simply good:
　　　　　　　ordinary people could finally leave
where they were born
and travel. Some diseases died. John
Lennon singing. About three hundred
good movies. The complexities
of new thought — Toni Morrison once noticing
that to read what Wittgenstein said
about colour is to
encounter poetry.

5.
You'll know more about images
than we do. But it was the twentieth century that made us live
pressed in between them like leaves
in a scrapbook. They're always
here. They eat

into us, keeping our nerves afloat while others manufacture

History with their bodies somewhere far away. The real images
are those you'll have to search for
yourself. Let your eyes play

with Man Ray, follow Orson Welles inventing the shadow, reach
into Nan Goldin's photos and feel how light is always
sweating because of its lust
to touch us.

6.
I started writing this poem when I was learning how

to talk. It's now the fortieth anniversary
of JFK in Dallas // And all I can remember of that Friday
are some broken waves in the back of my
head: a black and white TV screen; Kentucky Fried Chicken; it was

the very first time my grownups — Daddy, Mommy, my
beloved Grandmother (born Phoebe Kitely 1903 -
1966) — gave off something bad; something that night
was overwhelming and wrong. And now, this anniversary
weekend in 2003 they keep
                              playing the scene: a boy salutes
his Daddy going by in a colourful
coffin. That boy became a man and he'd be my age
now, except

he died pointlessly in an airplane crash — & was anything
in his life
as important as that ancient gesture made
when he was three?

7.
Now you're four and seven — too young for all of this, too young
too for me to have left you and your Mom
in September. I don't know, I just don't know
how you're going to remember this alien
and abrupt time. Will you
remember that I came to your home often — to tell you
stories in my Captain Hook voice, to play the game
we invented
using coloured sponge balls — to try to explain why

I'm renting this room that's mostly scattered paper, a few toy
birds, and a blue spider resting on top of a black
Derby hat. It perplexes you

when I tell you that my apartment has only
a bed, a chair, and a table, but no TV. And no, I don't
get lonely. But Mommy does, you
say. And my incomparable

daughter knows about poems / she showed me the poem she wrote
    about bats
at Halloween. And she wants to know exactly when
I'll be finished writing poems, when I'll finally
come home / and
then she fires her silver bullet, the one that finds
its place inside me when
she asks — But Daddy are poems more important
than I am?

8.

9.
It's not really like that
I say after a long time, but my

Darling, you were sleeping, and
I walked and walked some more to find
this place so I could tell you about a few things

that shaped and disappeared
from your Mom and Dad, and the other

big people around you — all of us who
will never touch who
you really are

SCIENCE SOLVES MUNCH'S MOST FAMOUS PAINTING

For Don Coles

The sky is wrong.

During that twilight in 1883, a shoal of salmon found slaughter
in the sharpened clouds. Blinded by fire, a moth then envisions
thousands of poppies in battered fields
yet to come. The sky's a venereal wound as wide
as God's absent gaze. *All*

at once the sky became blood-red, Munch
wrote, I stood alone trembling
with anxiety. I felt
a great unending scream
piercing through nature. But we've

2.

refashioned what cut through Munch and banished
it to gift shops. The nineteenth century and its silhouettes
crowded round the abyss have been paved over
with cellophane. We've finally discovered how art can become
something useful. My key

chain's a plastic copy of the central figure in "The Scream." It feels
nice, the size of a small cock in my pocket, nestled
there with my change. The volcano did it / or at least

that's what one of today's newspapers says — *Volcano*
created The Scream's "clouds of blood": scientists
maintain. Astronomers in Texas have sewed 1883
into one world. A volcano erupted in Indonesia, Krakatoa, and
immediately emptied itself into Edvard Munch's Norwegian
eye. Burned there for almost a decade

and then became the bloody
ejaculate the painter eventually
made, showing precisely the moment when Nature finally
broke apart, felt judged, and tore
itself then into a voice. But we've lost

patience with visible sounds, have soothed aside
the world with
our many narratives / they're ribbons
we use to tie things back together again / they're fables whose fright
anchors them within the simple
causalities. But art
historians don't care

about the volcano's haphazard
death drive; they want to know what it was
that blew apart inside Munch when he finally painted
the picture in '91. It was because

3.
Nature takes a long time to deliver
its dead. Beneath such a sky, eight years can
be a lifetime. It was because it took Munch
that long to get really fucking tired of people always insisting
you're one of us; you can keep trying, but you'll never
get out or away. Open

a door. Walk along a skeletal road. Squeeze bedtime's
toothpaste — it never
goes away.

What?
The lake.
Which lake?

The one they're always digging up. The one
in which science uncovers mere history, and only
yesterday, we rode and rode, feeling for a dead
purpose, but could only find one gesture
to remember. Except

4.
the world's already always the same. The same
front page in the newspaper tells how a woman
in a car crash caused by the random stupidity of weather
died Monday night

after doctors delivered her baby girl; she's 14 weeks
premature. And the world's never once the same — so many
things can never return to where they once
would have belonged.

5.
Twenty years ago, Don Coles gave a few of us a tour of a dozen
artists who worked against some corners in the sockets
of the skull. Chipped away there. Tore apart
the amazing, intersected
past. Malcolm Lowry. Munch. Adrienne
Rich. His own quiet voice. Little made
sense then, but I remember his hand
on my shoulder on one of my more
difficult Friday mornings — so recently
wifeless, wifeless for the first time, so little

left over inside. Only a few months ago
I was in Oslo, once Christiania, and went
to the Munch museum (with my key chain in
my pocket) and held some of *Forests of the Medieval
World,* poems by Don Coles, in the back

of my head. Don't merely look at the women, he'd
said, watch the brother, too, the way he makes the private
self an arrow, the way

the brother then made his way into my hotel
room filled with telephone lines, a toy unicorn, and those seductive
and graceful and damaging
nights. Norwegian

women are always rising from a bath, even
when they're glancing at the exact chair that held
Munch's sister as she was
finding her endlessly repeated
grave. Everything's been
seen before, and so it was only Munch's photos, I mean

6.
the ones he'd made himself, that
I was able to see, that found
me admitting my stupidity. It
was the one he'd taken of
a naked model, the one who's blurred between
her sloping skin and the obscene ghost in
a nightshirt behind her. I read her name as
she walked across the room
in the photograph, but who

is she? Who *is* she — this blunt and sleepless
woman who makes each of us a spinning
Eurydice unable to stop the headless and
greening light? Expressionist precision turns
the word *bereft* into a web strewn across
the volcanic. Lonely.

8.
Paltry. And not unreasonably, two figures walk apart
from Nature's painted howl, unseeing, and
one of us — oblivious — and they're both loosely pondering if
the day couldn't be a better one, if only someone fun
you can't remember yet
would somehow come along. Well. We

keep longing within a sunken
totality, and we keep speaking into ourselves, and we reach
for another's hand as we
walk along the crowding
ridge of the unheard.

LOVES

FOUR WINDOWS

I live behind four windows.

1.
Out of one
the way the irresistible world looks —

the red shafted flicker, a male, its inaudibly long
beak finding ant upon ant on the edge of the driveway, clouds
the precise metal of those disinfectant trays
people step in before swimming, the radiance of

children's toothpaste. Not seeking
beauty only, this window
needs the pearl of vindication.

2.
But there's another window, this one
impossible — the long ago April afternoon when

no one was looking, and I put on my new
tiger striped hat, my six foot feather boa, mostly
blood red, and then some blue lipstick
to hand out ceramic dragons and Batman nightlights
at my son's fourth birthday party / and uneasy, he
needed to know
                    You're still my Dad, aren't you?

My children, their hungered, and unjustly

bountiful looking into a man
who then learned how to elude things.

3.
Almost, but not yet, I'm almost the age
at which most of my dead
haven't died from suicide. They, my dead, bend

the glass of that window there, the one that moves, that keeps
slipping while turning itself toward me.

4.
An ocean is adjacent to the fourth window.

Because the waves are abandoned nowadays, of the four
windows
       this is the one I press against,
                      touching
the glass, its vertical slope, this thin place where
moments and love and the irrevocable
began.

TO MY FIRST LOVE

I'm sorry for falling away from you last night on the telephone
but I was brokenly dreaming. It's
been twenty years and

I'm still here, still chained to nicotine, unwhispered
temptations. Still seek the welcoming glitter of gas stations,
deepened by a night of endless driving, a woman's
bare foot resting on the dash. Many thousands of young
and older words ago, I pretended to be sleeping, with my fingers
combing your pubic hair, teasing out the threads
the Aegean's jelly fish had left there. Pink
negligee. Your fingerprint goes
here:

This isn't what I'd choose to tell you, but steam
from the dryers in the basement is drifting up like dry ice and
in the midst of this temporary fog
some poor bastard's beating his Xmas
tree to death over the hood of a stranger's car. It must

be the gray-green wind. Or perhaps it's the two moons, finally appearing
together, girlish and unequal, one brilliant, cold confidence,
the lesser one muted, the pewter-coloured earring
worn by Kepler's servant. The past,

my ancient darling, is oceanic and suddenly
undisturbed — a Faustian drug with only
two side effects: Compassion.
Denial.

THE ANIMALS

My daughter lost a word yesterday,
animals are no longer *aminals*, animals
have become what they should be, and
then she tried to straighten her brother out, welcome
him into our human pack, but he's sticking
to what he knows.

Because there's no word that holds what passed between
them in their car seats I've taken some toys
and lined them up by the window pane:

a yellow-billed pelican with blurred pink eyes, a hard
rubber ball with a fairy inside, a soldier aiming
and a petite Socrates that somehow came
in a box of plastic ancient things:

more warriors, a kneeling knight, heading off to Palestine, the other
a Samurai, and then a deep-sleeved Sage, a dark lidded
mummy too, asleep inside its hands-crossed, cobra-hooded
sarcophagus. And then this morning

my only son and daughter undid everything, so now
there's simply the pelican rammed up against
the philosopher, and the soldier raising his rifle above
a red fire engine. But my

darlings, because there's no word that shows
how shadows on evening snow
have even more shadows
hiding inside them, and because
there's never enough words
for what surrounds you as you sleep

and because tonight the trees are cracking
dark constellations, the winds jibbering among
summer's faraway garden statues, I've come again
to this random place, this home here
where I kill old poems, all the many
old poems, and I'm troubled
because so often, my

                  angels,
there's not enough food, not enough
and then each kind of animal
begins its roving.

THIS AFTERNOON

we're in the park throwing some pennies once
more into the magic fountain, magic because at Christmas
the water's somehow turned into falling loops
and stranded archways — a precise havoc
of happy streaming electric lights.

The stone fish who live here all year round

like the summer best we
decide. And then one of the new
fathers goes running by, pushing someone in a slick
three wheeler, a drag racer burning up the path, and my son (four
this month) wants to know: when I become a baby again
can you get me
one of those?

His sister jumps in, tells him he'll never be a baby
again, but O God, neither of them
sees the distance taking shape
in her news. Until then

I'd thought he'd taken mostly
after his mother / our daughter,
me. Once

she stalled me when out of a chaos
of letters   she formed her first

correctly spelled word: *cat*. And
a bubble cracked inside showing me

showing my mother a mad map of paper
with the word *cat* on it, just like
hers, wrestled from a child's magic
marker cabbala / a fluke

                no doubt. But tonight
I'm looking out of my old bedroom window, it's another
afternoon, a Sunday in August I think. I'm twelve again

for the first time, and there's some guys I've never
liked playing street hockey, and I'd been waiting

for the moment when it would
all begin again, when this watery

life would finally start for real — so that twelve years
later I'd find myself exactly twelve
again looking out my bedroom
window / and I find Mom
in the far away

kitchen down the hall. She's canning and I sit
cross legged on the floor, look up (the
Portuguese rooster's still there) and ask her if life happens
twice — would we be going to the beach again someday
the same way we'd done last weekend? When does
everything come back? But I didn't really
need to ask, I already half / knew
what she'd say.

            And so, tonight
my heart is travelling
in flame — what made him, what made
my son see the perfect ride and want
to make sure that when he became
a baby again that it
would be his?

Perhaps everyone feels the sift
of metaphysics, except
my daughter already knows
it's not like that. This

then is my prayer — may neither
of them choose to see how
appealing it is to take a fingernail
and slice open the present
to find what's missing in the long rooms
there.   Let them find instead

their mother's voice
listening, always listening, the way
she listens inside them.

I'm growing very fond of the yellow hard
hats those men are wearing across
the vacant lot: small spheres of yellow, always moving. The dance
of bees. There are so few different
colours here. Where
I used to live

elderly women walk embroidered dogs beneath amber / pink
     streetlamps.
Houses keep them. Roads curve. Red-breasted nuthatches
fly through tunnels of air. Here the old learn

the endless line of sidewalk with the slow infinity
of canes. It's October. And most mornings,
a distracted man paces the lobby with bare
feet, nervous about snow. The halls are
crammed with other people's dying
meals. People here are
dwarves who make their way
to a shopping mall built

for others. Plastic grocery bags become
purses and other tools. They also decorate
the scarce trees in the pavement. People
in the next apartment are knocking
teeth out with a hair dryer. First his, then
hers, then just the wall; it's so very

hard to decide

where anything is.

A DAY IN THE MORNING

Kafka once mentioned that to waken
and find the space around you,
its daylight-thickened objects,
to find them the same as the night before
is the deepest amazement.
Nothing that follows can equal
that first astonishment.

Like everything Kafka said, this is as true as an envelope. But

long into this morning — just beside
the elevator and behind a door, a man with emphysema
was watching a video of reruns of great moments
in hockey. Here we go again, the voiceover
said, and this man behind the door
clapped to each dead hockey moment, breathed
with lungs of wet stone, and he said
oh yeah, oh yeah, oh yeah. What becomes

more to the point than trying to understand
how pleasure drifts in the cocoons of
other people? Find out
whether pleasure is repetition only or a surprise
coming across midnight's periphery? Because
I didn't need to go anywhere, because
I've severed ties with urgency, I returned
to my room. Besides, Franz, it's snowing like hell
on this the first real storm of the year. The snow

is blowing not down, but prairie flat, horizontal along the wind, something
you may not have seen in Prague. And Franz, for years
I've never been sure what waking up actually means. A jeep
skids beneath the angel blur and then a woman
in the parking lot starts waving something like a net from
a fishing trawler. It's huge above her — she's trying to hold
everything in. She must be asleep somewhere
and dreaming herself into this scene; but there she is, and I think
she should begin seeing someone about her dreams.

I bought two things yesterday:

A toy black panther whose eyes search
out mine, and sometimes I love
this world very much, but
then Karl Marx looks at me from the newspapers
I no longer read. I turn the panther over, tickle
his silly sharp belly, and he was made
in some life-flattening factory in
China — this reminder

of Rilke would make Marx rage, or
weep, or deny the fireworks sound, the meaningless
air of History. Franz, my heart doesn't
have as many vacated rooms as

yours did, but I also bought a small square
of sparkled gray felt yesterday for the woman
I left because I've needed for a long time
to do more than accost familiar strangers
in the subway that home became. And
somewhere in her life across the snow

this morning, right now, this very snow, she's woken to
find herself become a jewelry store set on fire by
thieves. For the hundredth time now, each morning she wakes to this
dull fire. And so do our children.

The felt looks like an ocean floor; it's to give
her feet a place to rest on. I'd settle

for anything if there could be a passage
between pop sickle night
and panegyric day — the automatic writing between them, the green
glow-in-the-dark makeup I use
when I'm walking beside my daughter. In her high chair, teenage boots,
and the voodoo flowers she'll one day

throw over me to seal me in. You'd agree, Franz that

so little is ever done, or well done, or even
attempted. Franz, the world's a transparent umbrella. We hold
this umbrella to ward off
what? Franz,
what? Tell me
once again.

HER SIDE

It's not true

Love that I'm wearing a wig — how do these
rumours ever start? I'm sorry, too, that I sometimes
close my eyes. But you and I, we've lived

many lives. The difference is I remember
all of them and you have trouble

keeping track of even one promise. You keep spilling
into either sleep or fury. When you do
look at me I'm invisible or a Gorgon. But last night
as you slept I kept watching the road of cars
beneath us. Their taillights were playful

and plastic rubies, except you weren't
here to share
these ordinary miracles. You keep

missing me. You didn't see me lift a strip of concrete
sidewalk from the street down there. It was the size
of an air mattress, and I lay it on the carpet, took
off my dress, and posed on top of it like a pin up
floating
in a swimming pool in some mechanic's garage.

Keep your bitterness to yourself. Don't
get angry again. I'm not
a cage. Though it
feels like I'm being kept
in one. And I'm tired

of taping your wrists back together with cellophane, am
tired, too, of pulling each day we spend together out of
my cunt like it's a string
of razor blades and pearls
for tourists. The disasters you think you feel
are nothing, nothing, they're cartoons

compared to what you've made me become.

You can't see that we don't live
anywhere anymore. We're
not even ghosts. We're
not even the history
of a simple crime. We're
just monsters you've
imagined — all
by yourself — not real at
all, but wearisome and vicious

all the same. Please
stop. You've promised
you'd never look at me
that way again.

THE GROCERY STORE IS WILLING TO SELL

Us
everything.

I choose the usual fruit, the Mexican
refried beans you love (just in case you
drop by someday), Puritanical celery
and cigarettes, walk away from the many
ways you can eat chicken, the wintergreen
chewing gum. I'm looking

for eye-glass cleaner, having broken down
finally — I've got one bottle in my office, another
at my ex-wife's, but I need one I can carry
with me. My face sweats so much sometimes it's
like snails are copulating on the lenses. The bosc pear
is a freckled green and brown breast — perfect for
my camera later. There are enough toothbrushes
to polish the boots of every cop in a city
larger than this one. Condoms, I discover, are more
detailed and energetic than when I first bought them.

What's different today is the woman who entered
the store behind me: she's been leading
a blind man with a grocery cart
and just now he's following her voice
through a canyon that leads to milk
and his favourite cheese. I feel
a little odd when I see the lens
cleaner in my basket, but this kind
of irony is lazy; it's fastening a constellation
onto what isn't there. When

I leave the store I glance at the newspaper headlines:
some roofers in Montreal were burnt alive yesterday
while tarring a roof. A teenage boy
told the reporter that they
looked like stuntmen in a movie.

2.

I've been to Montreal, licked so much wine
off a woman there the sheets looked
as if a sweating Dionysos had made the bed
his nest. I've also worked on a flat roof
with steaming tar a dozen floors
above the ground; it's hard, evil
smelling, and dirty work.
Even after a shower, small leopard spots stick
to your skin. It's true too

that a poem should amble between images, should
contain as many vowels and hard, surrendered
velvets as a grocery store holds food
and other things that sleep

until someone chooses to buy them. Sometimes
I believe that the only honest
writing is the list: pear, blind man, death in
a shit job. Unsmudged
glasses. But I've

been home now for over an hour, noticed folks
carrying plastic bags filled with what they like, or
need. Did anyone notice me doing the same thing, notice my
Our Lady Peace toque, divine what I was carrying
in my loosened head? Someone has thrown

a smoke onto the road. Someone else just
emptied a cauldron above me off
the apartment roof — what's coming down
are all the days those men in Montreal
will never live to ignore. The spew
is translucent, almost lemon, something

tender and savage, something that
will never mean much
to the rest of us as we
continue leaving grocery stores
with what we're strong enough
to carry home with our hands. Only you
can see inside to these disasters

of timing. Tell me, will

3.
you bring the fangs I sent
you when you visit me? You can
wear them safely. I poured boiling
water over them before I placed
them in the envelope. Be careful, though, be careful

with the way you approach the words you find
yourself having to use. Words want
to be touched — sometimes
with talons, sometimes with
a geisha's hands. If angered, words
will make light bulbs explode
in your apartment, leaving tiny tungsten wires hanging down
like the poison negligee jelly fish thread just beneath

the sea's surface
after a storm.

4.

I've bought some small swans and a wandering string
of pearls to play with you, placed
the swans on the window ledge beneath a Black Maria
playing card. And on the wall I've glued
a woman who is as voiceless
as a giraffe as she inserts a candle into her nineteenth-
century quim. When words eventually come to her she
tells me about the future

rising behind me, the one
I can't begin to see because of my
specific past. People there, I'm told, have

orchestras shaking inside them, and entire
populations line the edges of high rises to watch
a new species endlessly divide within
the amazed air, and nothing, I'm
told, is left unclaimed.

AUBADE

The street lamps are just beginning
their daylight faces, and I've already
awoken several times to find
myself eating my way out
of swollen zebra bellies, stuffed birds, even
tree trunks — this is
not being beside you. When
I was I was

infinite. The past is unequally peopled, the present, an
airplane caught on a sunflower, the future, a door
into a hall filled with chairs.

Plain talk.

You fed me lox, called me your
wide-eyed and babbling goy, gave me
a camel's bone for strength (one
you'd been keeping for yourself), lit vanilla
candles with your voice.

On top of your small body I showed
you how to play slow and spooky
Tarot with postcards we stole
from the art museum. Giacometti.
Steiglitz. Sasabuchi. Munch.

A Schiele that couldn't quite
contain your pussy's spill. The Magritte
no one has ever seen, the one sprung
from the good streets of your past in Montreal: there's
a man — he's taking his hat

for a walk today; he's turned once
in your direction, right there in the field, snapped
open his favourite calculator just to watch
how numbers form and then
they disappear again.

The sky soon will be the bluest of scarves and one day
I'll run its silk over you.

Everything will stagger if I can't.

Plainer talk. Trees are shaking. Somewhere
a hummingbird's wings are moving
so quickly they could be a line
a pencil might draw across
the air.

Look into a mirror to see you
for me.

Nothing anyone could ever tell you
will undo your surprise
at living among other
people. And

you are there.

And I'm here.

ADUMBRATION

Nothing remembers the continuous.

When you're not here I write to you with a wren's eye.
And all night I hear woodcutters, even when
I'm not sleeping — muted gray
breaking on solid black. When you're

not here not a single car has passed
by in over a century. Except the dragonfly
taxis ferrying the dead to the prairie / or
wherever it is they must go. When you're not here

my arms have turned into a carpenter's saws,
metal limbs incapable of touch or
the gambols of flight.

Imagine if you had to see the world only through a child's toy
    telescope.

The sky's been taken apart.
Its sun is everywhere, a sunken aviary of light.

What I mean is that nothing assuages the continuous.
What I mean is that I mean all of this.

You're both David and Bathsheba.
When you're not here our skin forgets how to speak, and we both
have to relinquish

what's nearby
differently.

A FIVE-YEAR OLD WITH SCISSORS

Must have made the sky today. Don't

stir from the sheets; you can't tell
from the light what time it is. It could
be morning. It could
still be tomorrow. There must

be a parade coming. In threes and fours, a crowd's ambled past
carrying lawn chairs that could just as easily
be suitcases or windowpanes.

When it rains, each drop is the world wanting
to be heard. And when a woman cums, each sound
is time learning
how to speak. I'm not

afraid of you any more.

Said the aphorism
to the dictionary. Said failure
to its white shadow
always dogging along

behind. I'm learning to restrain
my harsher judgments. It's not as though
I carried anyone on the back of my bicycle
to escape the burning towers.

> Things are right in front of us. Why make them up?
>
> Jean Luc Godard
> *In Praise of Love*

1.

The radio has just mentioned that graffiti
is vandalism, not art. As a public service, Regina's Police Dept.
   will name
the stores that sell the best solvent for removing it.
Graffiti, that is, not
vandalism, nor art. Perhaps it's because I got my eyelid
tattooed by the ghost of Basquiat, Jean-
Michel, when the woman (I always
wanted) packed up that I've become
scissor / serious about garage doors, rattlesnake
windows, and what could happen to the sky / if vandals, or
artists were let loose —

2.

I keep finding things in Zip-lock bags:
   a) an American Goldfinch feeding on black stars
   b) the moment Joseph Cornell discovered the work of William
      Harnett
   c) an eagerness to bring Ruskin in / but not yet / this is supposed
      to be a narrative poem
   d) a Zip-lock bag that contains within it at least four other bags,
      one holding a stone that's only a stone, another an eye-print
      from a cyborg, kept fresh from TV, a further, the complicated
      happiness

of Saturday, August 13, 2005 — when

we lay in your new bed, after a walk, a Breakfast Special, a used
book store (I found some Ruskin, Scribner's, 1918, you a stamp with
Hitler's face on it, 1938), and the clouds turning two waterfalls into
afternoon sleep; and last night we had sex, mostly with our hands,
and through the night, morning and early afternoon, exhausted

from her M.S., her drugs and O.C.D., your visiting mother still
snores in the next room / she's sleeping off

the dinner I made last night (a version of Napoleon's Chicken
Marengo), and Cronenberg's movie about a man who knew
he was a spider, but was confused about mothers
and the complications of killing people
like them. And during the meal, your Mom was
a set of ruins
      remarkable in their after glow / you could see
what she'd once been when she wanted to talk
about what it is that people
need / you offered
the story of Lear, a man she'd once
heard of

back before the brain-wearying shark of her diseases set in / and I'm
  left wondering if she finds
anything within her life to be anything
close to holy

3.
We lay in bed, two waterfalls; but after awhile
you drove me back here, to where we used
to live until I hurt you into leaving / and

I read two newspapers that afternoon, dipped into the Ruskin, turned
on the radio, and then tried to teach myself
to speak Elephant, and I need to eat and I need to avoid
becoming prey and things are right
in front of us — why make
them up?

4.
"It's basically about art, I'm an artist," says Dr. David Matlock, cosmetic
surgeon, tagged the Picasso of vaginas.* And why
not, if art improves on life, creates new
beauty, and reshapes our shifting
origins? The times
change, but

time does not. Ruskin, I find, is
a gorgeous genius of
graffiti, spraying

his pain across disappearing crowds
and decades / and John, here's what
we both need:
more than a dozen
cans of spray paint / and before us
a naked cathedral —

---

*   See Jill Mahoney, "Designer vaginas: the latest in sex and plastic surgery,"
    The Globe and Mail, 13 Aug. 2005, p. A8.

5.
I've listened to a sky, the first one, the one before
God decided to make

the one on top
of us. And waited

and watched. And done whatever it is that sallies
between the two. And I've kept
count of things:

It takes God nine glasses of vodka, each filled with fire flies, to move
from one creature to the next, trying to invent
a new kind of life each and every
impossible time (by the time

he got to us he would cross every edge
wavering in front and
all around him)

6.
                What joy there was
when the dragonfly first perched on his finger for warmth —

its many-veined wings in the light, hundreds
of carnivorous lakes all flashing guitar
crazy in the sun's water and the water's sun

its four wings
sparkling
the future's stained glass, the lights
of every city seen
from the air at night,

7.
and then God caught me
looking, not
at him,

      but for you,
amy, for
you.

CONVERSATIONS

COLLECTING

> The collector's impulse does not encourage the lust to understand or to transform. Collecting is a form of union. The collector is acknowledging. He is adding. He is learning. He is noting.
>
> Susan Sontag
> *The Volcano Lover*

Gets off his bike, he's scavenging
butts from ashtrays adrift outside
office buildings, those foreign
islands wavering just beyond
the shark in his blood; his is
a hunger of which I can only dream.

Removes his earphones, says he has epsy, and They won't
let him get any jobs — do I know of any good jobs?

He doesn't like AC/DC and all that bad screaming, though
Guns N' Roses are perfect, perfect and then he's off again, protected
by combat pants, by music and
abandoned treasure and disappearing /

it's so good —
disappearing into
the aimless dark.

2.
I hoard the usual stuff.

Bottles of antique vitamins, fresher aspirin, light and other loves held
in photographs, a leg — all that's left of a doll I crucified

in childhood. A pop can tab a woman asked me to keep
safe for her when she again went travelling; she'd pulled it from
a baby's throat when she'd worked
in an orphanage down south. Some aventurine
glass buttons — fossilized sunrise over the Atlantic before
people had learned to fly — and a Bodhisattva

coated with my daughter's nail polish. A reproduction of
Michelangelo's *Rage* over my door, its countless lines a sea
swirling into two small caves — the eyes — and
the mouth's whirlpool
of negation. A film canister filled

with small gray stones — my sister took them
from the parking lot crammed with tour buses outside a Zen garden
in Kyoto, though I'd clearly asked
her for some sand the monks have spent centuries raking away
into what's never sufficiently here / and I have eight
clocks, one

flesh pink squid, the thousand books, the invisible griefs and
guilts from abandoning married life
to live like a skeleton in a Halloween display.

                                        I have

too many masks because people think
I collect wooden masks / and then
there's also the dancer lying on
the floor — these

are the myriad stolen and rampant things that pass
through smudged glass without anyone knowing
how
to make an account.

INTERRUPTIONS

Rainer Maria Rilke slipped on some stairs yesterday —
the ice of the casino world
beneath him.

2.

But today, angry with himself over women, and
the echoes of other people delaying
the present, its leftover words, today
he's visited the zoo to watch the angles
and long orbits fish make when
they live behind glass. The strict
and communal world: a damselfish with one socket
eaten away

into tattered pink, the other eye, black, abrupt
and tapering / dreamless / both fastened upon
this untoward man who knows
his muscles have never moved
like the panther's. Human, his arms and legs are like the trees arranged
outside the zoo's pavilions — the day's limbs are blind and necessary
arteries. Scratch

that. Start over. Trees are excess without parallel
                    for birds
to divide the immediate — a sky
of travellers and shifting birth. But us?

Our proteins to give voice to the brisk and answer-less
world? The invisible needs to become
our voice?   Tonight, Rilke
is no longer quite so sure.

3.

A coat on the floor. A hat on the door. The wine
winos drink in Rilke's glass. Ancient cigarette
burns on the fresh sheets behind him. Make believe exile
in a hotel only the relentless would
choose for a holiday.

Places have always kept him spellbound. Nearby's

a railway. The sun-chipped sidewalks are nothing to the missing cats
and dogs. In this city, trains only slow down and sometimes pause.
Guarding the airport's exit is an enormous grasshopper covered in
plants. The Plains Hotel has been remodelled. But it still sports a
small tower that looks like a spinal column dwindling upwards, its
vertebrae a memorial to the short supply of grandeur. That one place

isn't another has always nourished
his determination.

At night, Rilke can remember what didn't happen
to him in this room: he sees that a woman has
howled because of the way a man
has watched a television.

4.
Each of us tries out the rules of chess: discern

your opponent's thinking; outguess it, dampen
the despair
choice brings. Observe

5.
the urge to forfeit everything.

6.
Because the gods offer us addictions — the vine,
the home — just so we can taste what
they've left behind.

> The genuine method of considering the world philosophically,
> in other words, that consideration which acquaints us with
> the inner nature of the world and thus takes us beyond the
> phenomenon, is precisely the method that does not ask about
> the whence, whither, and why of the world, but always and
> everywhere about the what alone.
>
> > Arthur Schopenhauer
> > *The World as Will and Representation*

The first task is to settle on just what the hell
is here — leave the rest. Let others sew facts into stories
or plummet the why by tugging test tubes or
the cross. And if the first task is endless, that's our burden, not
our guilt, we merely found ourselves in the world's
eyes. Except, Arthur, only days ago a man fell
from space, Arthur, an astronaut, the shuttle exploding
mostly on TV, killing everyone within. His mother
survived Auschwitz; the explosion also destroyed a Torah
taken into space, one left over from the same camp that killed
Anne Frank, whose diary the astronaut probably had read as a boy.
What is this, Arthur, this thing that's now
remaining behind?

The *Will*, you tell me, the blind, devouring Will pushes the sky
aside, bulldozes the earth with children. And I can't quarrel
with what you see. Some nights after the accident
I was walking home, it was late, after 1, and the sky
was a Rothko — city light orange / pink fleeing
into more kinds of black, some drier
than inky coal — and then I ate some chicken salad, read

a newspaper account of Ilan Roman* the astronaut, when my son cried
out in the dark having thrown up all over himself and his Batman
bed sheets, and I washed him, told
his Mommy to go back to bed, then held his shoulders
in the bathroom, knew that Ilan's mother had once

held him the same way and that her mother had done this for her
     years before
the camps. If to see these things is our burden what I cannot do
is say precisely what is here; I can only
work easy narrative, tell you:
and this and this and then. Arthur, I too distrust
emotion, have no faith in whys, refuse
the partisan gloss — accidents inherited from
not even thirsty time — but always and everywhere
indifferent details hunt for us. Yesterday

I took my kids to an arcade. After we'd played, shot
aliens, drove imaginary race cars, we exchanged the tickets we'd won
for a bracelet with Oriental writing on it, candy, plain
potato chips, a toy jeep. For me, a pair of green eyes in paper
glasses because behind my plastic framed glasses
rest my own green eyes; and I can't account
for them, details, I mean, what lives inside them, what
escapes, which green eyes we recognize watching
us because always and everywhere
details go after us.

---

* The phrase "a man fell from space," and the biographical information on
Ilan Ramon, are derived from a newspaper article. See Margaret Wente,
"The man who fell from space," *The Globe and Mail*, 4 Feb., 2003, p. A17.

2.

art, on the contrary, is everywhere at its goal. For it plucks the
object of its contemplation from the stream of the world's
course, and holds it isolated before it. This particular thing,
which in that stream was an infinitesimal part, becomes for art
a representative of the whole, an equivalent of the infinitely
many in space and time. It therefore pauses at this particular
thing; it stops the wheel of time; for it the relations vanish; its
object is only the essential, the Idea.

The World as Will and Representation

Art escapes relations, truly discards them back
from where they came into wavering form, but time

has never

been a wheel, time only factors
DOESN'T all the time. Art a part

of the whole, an equivalent

for the multi-variegated many? No one knows, no one

has ever left

the first cave, the first painting there, the hand reaching
out to stone, the hand reaching out to the last drawing of the earth
made by a boy dead in Theresiendstadt. And your lovely

sentences, Arthur — we

pick up words like stones because
poems are broken things, look at

that man

asleep on a ledge, he's restless, he's holding
evergreens, their gray light, their steady
gray, inner light, its corners, secret
from the snow

the watchful snow —
when something akin
to the Minotaur bursts
through.

INSIDE THE DOG PARK

for Frida (½ border collie, but mostly sentient wind)

A dog barked, whined as if a beater had given him a whack,
then barked again. The barking of the dog, a protest against the
limits of dog experience (for God's sake, open the universe a
little more!) —

Saul Bellow
The Dean's December

Bellow's dead now. But I've been
thinking of that dog that once barked metaphysical rebellion in
broken Chicago. And today, I've wished
him here
in the dog park. Regina's recently

2.
given up some of its prairie
for unleashed dogs
to run across. Niagara
Falls — humans place words

on top of space, I tell Frida (named after
the painter) — Frida, this dog park is huge, it could easily be
the flattened spray of Niagara Falls, X5, if drained

across trodden and thistled grass, reincarnated
sunsets. But you,

Frida, running an eclipse without planets, or tapered
moons, or anything that's without
freedom, first,

you stop
and look back to make sure I'm still in range / and then you let me know

that no one can identify
what continuity
actually is. There's

3.
paws and froth and deciding
who's boss upon each and every
ready encounter / there's life
on four legs lived
invisibly — these dogs leap
from Pompeii —

                      cave canem, as
abandoning form / these dogs, each with three, maybe five
bodies apiece, know the trick is to collide without once

losing your ground / and these dogs
know what fences do, but not
what they're for / these fences
at

the prairie's edge
where the sky is
the same blue / gray
as the numbers
tattooed in their ears. I'd like

4.
to invite Kurulek back
from the dead to paint this
place, take it in.
In. Inside

         his sudden glance, joy's

a reasoning
phantom, always burrowing out
& into the light. His eyes'

lungs would love
it here: the few

trees that dogs love to piss against; the big-
breasted, small woman
in her brilliant red hat — the way
that people
are mostly the coats they
wear. The
            unnecessary clouds, a needle to the creek's
intelligible thread. No one
listens

4.
as well as a painter does and Kurulek,

back from the dead, keeps repeating
that there's only one
currency — the baring
of teeth and the command
to look:

Now.

AMONG PAINTINGS

Mater Dolorosa and Christ Crowned With Thorns
From the workshop of Dieric Bouts, 1485-95

The eyes? The hands? Which loneliness
do you choose? Mary must watch
her son die. She must only
watch.

His hands have long nails, dirty, the fingers, each
an independence forming, if not a whole,
a way of joining things together.

This is before the cross.
Then fingers become irrelevant.

Mary's hands, still here over the centuries, are frost
bitten with care. His

are cradled together; they're the untroubled
ghosts that haunt seashells. Un-nailed, these hands
in the painting must surely belong
to someone else, perhaps to
the painter. Whose hand held brushes instead
of wind, magic bread and fish, iron.

Neither the son nor the mother
look at us directly; they are far away
from what paintings can show.

We can
see their tears. Mary's,
like droplets
of uncanny glass, his
bloody kerosene. Belong. Paintings change

our sense of belonging, turn us
into exacting strangers. We
see things that then
genuinely disappear.

2.

   Skeletons in the Studio
   James Ensor, 1900

This painting, dismemberment poured
through the telephone, is the one
of which I'm most afraid. Paintings

damage verbs. Self-knowledge is
two dimensional. Orpheus:
Jerry Lewis. A rhino can be made out of what light bulbs
can do.

A painted studio stuffed with painted objects. A skull
on a dwarfed body with something thick in its mouth. A dark screen
of birds. What does it mean
to create beauty? Suicide by entering a window
into, not out
of, a room. Hello?

Hello? Everything replies: Is

anyone there? Your portfolio is bloated next
to the palette on the floor. They
contain all four worlds. *Tod* isn't
only the snapping of fingers.

She crammed our names into a heart
beneath a bridge but had already
decided to leave me nights
before when we drove around
a Belgian lake, sat a statue of Freud on

a curbstone. Watched hawks hunt.

Your studio is blessed by enclosing that which doesn't
sleep — soup ladles, music, bits of the yellow
world, a fake statue
of the Virgin.

A perfect synthesis of associative thought.

Also a myriad of masks. One wearing blood like another
might grow a beard. Beneath it, a paper
slogan: *Mortes aux conformes.*

All of this a design on a shower curtain.

Swimmers; roses. Nothing

matters except the clawing
of greens you've

made the wall beside
the sky.

CODA: PLATO KNEW

That the shallows of autobiography
almost never occasion thought. Plato
knew that all of us, we're mostly
a rendezvous of coat hangers; their shadows
he meant. It can

be simple — merely take in the sun awakening
a patch, an aura, of dormant light
on this or any wall. But Plato
never gloried

in seeing you eat a mango, never met
thousands dead somewhere in a newspaper, hadn't felt
the bite a stalled car engine gives frozen fingers
in a snowstorm — one small
misery peculiar to our
time, this place.

And all of this, when the eyes clear —

2.
Christ, to find light's amber / last night's rain on
a warming sidewalk and beneath my eye
a wasp slides its needle into
a purse-black cricket — the
twist of venom and cloudy
ash —

A twig separates and startles them, but wasps
are insane. Flies back to kill some more.

As if my tennis shoe next achieved a kind
of unchosen and believing balance — by killing

them both, now

neither can be told apart any more.

3.
Children should be given peaches, toys, and barely
defined sports on fresh grass. Not

their mothers wearing intricate handkerchiefs
and breakable prayers outside a school's gymnasium
mined with explosives, trip wires that yesterday
a cow triggered in Russia, blew itself
apart on the unforeseen yard.

Poems shouldn't enter monochromatic politics, but
violence pushes everything aside to get
at the mere living.

And in each, a paucity
of deserving sounds. / The ABCs
of yellow and black and worn-out white

ACKNOWLEDGEMENTS

I would like to thank Don Coles for editing the ms. But my debt goes far beyond his precise eye, and wisdom, in editing; it was because of him and Eli Mandel, a very long time ago, that I first began to pay close attention to words. Almost every poem in this book attempts to say many things to both these poets, but "thank you" puts it most succinctly.

This collection couldn't have been written without Amy Snider, and Annie and Jesse Trussler. Only you will know what this means.

Friends over the years have offered encouragement and advice. Derek Brown, Paul Endo, Kat Nogue, Gillian Harding-Russell, Jeanne Shami, Dan Tysdal, and Kathleen Wall — you all have my gratitude. Andy Stubbs deserves special thanks for his constant willingness to look at yet another poem, and his wonderful suggestions. I also wish to thank Paul Wilson of Hagios Press for his support and editorial expertise — this book (and its title) are the result of his generosity — and Don Ward for the design and layout.

Many of the poems that have been edited for this collection have been previously published in the following journals and magazines: *The Antigonish Review*, *ARC*, *backwater review*, *CV2*, *Event*, *The Fiddlehead*, *Grain*, *The Malahat Review*, *The New Quarterly*, *Paperplates*, *Prairie Fire*, *PRISM International*, and *Vallum*.

AMY SNIDER

Michael Trussler was born in Kitchener, Ont., raised in New Hamburg, and currently lives in Regina. Sask. He earned a BA and an MA in English literature from York University, and a PhD from the University of Toronto. In 1997, he began teaching courses in American literature, literary theory, and the short story at the University of Regina. He has won three teaching awards, and is the editor of *Wascana Review*. He has published book reviews, literary criticism, poetry, and short fiction. He has travelled widely in the United States and Europe, is a father of two, an amateur photographer, and has a fascination with visual art. Michael Trussler's first book of short-fiction, *Encounters* (NeWest, 2006), was awarded both the Saskatchewan Book of the Year and the Regina Book Award at the 2006 Saskatchewan Book Awards.